Understanding God's W

Understanding
NORTH AMERICAN HISTORY

—A Christian Perspective—

Grade 8

Tests

Rod and Staff Publishers, Inc.
P.O. Box 3, Hwy. 172
Crockett, Kentucky 41413-0003
Telephone: (606) 522-4348

Copyright, 2005
by

***Rod and Staff Publishers, Inc.
Crockett, Kentucky 41413***

Printed in U.S.A.

ISBN 978-07399-0656-9
Catalog no. 19811

7 — 19

Front cover photograph used by permission from Mary Jane Auker.
Back cover photograph used by permission from Corel.

Understanding North American History

Chapter 1 Test

Name _____   Score _____   Date _____

A. Matching: Terms

Not all the choices will be used.

___ 1. Of the city.
___ 2. Low bowl-shaped area surrounded by higher land.
___ 3. High ridge that separates water flowing into the Pacific from water flowing into the Gulf of Mexico.
___ 4. Break in the earth's surface, where earthquakes occur.
___ 5. Permanently frozen soil.
___ 6. River that flows into a larger river.
___ 7. High, fairly level stretch of land.
___ 8. Place where water descends from the Piedmont to the lower Coastal Plain.
___ 9. Land formed by soil deposited at the mouth of a river.
___ 10. Broad bay at the mouth of a river.
___ 11. Long, narrow bay extending inland in a steep-sided valley.
___ 12. In contact; adjoining.
___ 13. Surface features of a region.

a. basin
b. contiguous
c. Continental Divide
d. delta
e. estuary
f. Fall Line
g. fault
h. fiord
i. permafrost
j. plateau
k. rural
l. topography
m. tributary
n. urban

(13 points)

B. Matching: Climates

___ 14. Sunny and mild; good for oranges and olives.
___ 15. Very warm and moist.
___ 16. Wet and mild; found in the Pacific valleys.
___ 17. Cold climate in Canada and Alaska.
___ 18. Climate of four seasons.

a. humid continental
b. humid subtropical
c. Mediterranean
d. subarctic
e. west coast marine

(5 points)

C. Matching: Features of the United States

Not all the choices will be used.

___ 19. Broad, flat region bordering the Atlantic Ocean and the Gulf of Mexico.

___ 20. Main features of the Pacific Coast region (3 answers).

___ 21. Main features of the Appalachian region (3 answers).

___ 22. Dry, low-lying area in the Rocky Mountain region.

___ 23. Highest mountain in the contiguous United States.

___ 24. Highest mountain in North America.

___ 25. River draining about 40 percent of the United States.

___ 26. Major tributary of the river in number 25.

___ 27. Volcanic islands in the Pacific Ocean.

___ 28. Long, wide mouth of the Susquehanna River.

___ 29. Salty body of water in the Great Basin region.

___ 30. Alaskan river flowing into the Pacific Ocean.

a. Allegheny and Cumberland Plateaus
b. Appalachian Mountains
c. Atlantic Coastal Plain
d. Chesapeake Bay
e. Coast Ranges
f. Columbia
g. Great Basin
h. Great Salt Lake
i. Hawaii
j. Mississippi
k. Missouri
l. Mt. McKinley
m. Mt. Whitney
n. Pacific ranges
o. Pacific valleys
p. Piedmont
q. St. Lawrence
r. Yukon

(16 points)

D. Matching: Features of Canada

Not all the choices will be used.

___ 31. River flowing from the Great Lakes to the Atlantic Ocean.

___ 32. Rocky region curving like a horseshoe around Hudson Bay.

___ 33. Vast stretch of level land in the central area.

___ 34. Heartland of Canada in Ontario and Quebec.

___ 35. Longest river in Canada.

___ 36. Region of the provinces along the Atlantic Ocean.

___ 37. Highest of the Canadian Rockies.

___ 38. Region including Rocky Mountains and Coast Ranges.

a. Appalachian region
b. Canadian Shield
c. Columbia
d. Cordillera region
e. Great Lakes-St. Lawrence Lowlands
f. Interior Plains
g. Mackenzie
h. Robson
i. St. Lawrence

(8 points)

E. Essay Questions

39. How are history and geography related?

_____

_____

_____

40. How has the climate of Canada affected the settlement of the nation?

_____

_____

_____

(2 points)
Total points: 44

Understanding North American History

Chapter 2 and 3 Test

Name _____

Score _____

Date _____

A. Matching: Terms—Chapter 2

Not all the choices will be used.

___ 1. Rebirth of learning.

___ 2. The East.

___ 3. Boundary drawn by the pope to give Spain rights to the New World.

___ 4. Viking settlement in North America.

___ 5. Person who invests money to make a profit.

___ 6. System in which a lord owned land, and serfs farmed it for him.

___ 7. People who were neither lords nor serfs.

___ 8. Island on which Columbus landed.

___ 9. Country for which Columbus sailed.

___ 10. Major change in the religious system of Europe.

a. capitalist
b. Line of Demarcation
c. manorialism
d. middle class
e. Orient
f. Portugal
g. Reformation
h. Renaissance
i. San Salvador
j. Spain
k. Vinland

(10 points)

B. Matching: Terms—Chapter 3

Not all the choices will be used.

___ 11. A particular way of life.

___ 12. Indian village of multilevel apartment houses made of stone or adobe.

___ 13. Crumbled meat mixed with buffalo tallow.

___ 14. Dwelling made of poles bent in a U shape and covered with bark.

___ 15. Bricks made of sun-dried clay.

___ 16. One of the old men who governed the Iroquois.

___ 17. Region where tribes lived similarly.

___ 18. Manmade object, such as a tool or weapon, that is of interest in archaeology.

___ 19. Pair of poles drawn by a dog or horse, used by Plains Indians to carry their belongings.

a. adobe
b. artifact
c. culture
d. culture area
e. longhouse
f. pemmican
g. pueblo
h. sachem
i. travois
j. wigwam

(9 points)

C. Completion: People—Chapter 2

Write the correct name for each description.

_____ 20. "Admiral of the Ocean Sea" who discovered the New World in 1492.

_____ 21. Explorer of the North American coast for France in 1524.

_____ 22. Italian for whom the lands of the New World were named.

_____ 23. Scandinavian explorer who reached the northeastern coast of North America around A.D. 1000.

_____ 24. Explorer of the northeastern coast of North America for England in 1497.

_____ 25. Captain of five ships, one of which became the first to sail around the world.

_____ 26. Explorer who claimed part of America for the Netherlands in 1609.

_____ 27. Scandinavian people who settled Iceland, Greenland, and Vinland around A.D. 1000.

_____ 28. Explorer of the St. Lawrence River area for France in 1534.

_____ 29. Explorer who discovered in 1513 that a great ocean lay west of America.

_____ 30. Explorer who reached the Orient by sailing around Africa.

_____ 31. Queen of Spain who financed Columbus's voyage of discovery.

(12 points)

D. Matching: Areas and Tribes—Chapter 3

____ 32. Area from North Carolina to the Gulf of Mexico and from the Atlantic Ocean to the Mississippi River.

____ 33. Area from the Mississippi River to the Rocky Mountains.

____ 34. Area in California, the Great Basin, and the Columbia Plateau.

____ 35. Area in present-day Arizona, New Mexico, and parts of Texas.

____ 36. Area between the Great Lakes and North Carolina.

a. Northeast
b. Southeast
c. Plains
d. Southwest
e. Far West

In the set below, choices may be used more than once or not at all.

____ 37. Culture that made heaps of earth for ceremonies and burial.

____ 38. Tribe that lived in pueblos.

____ 39. Tribe that lived in longhouses.

____ 40. Tribe that used kivas.

____ 41. Another name for Eskimos.

____ 42. Tribes called the Five Nations.

____ 43. Indians that lived in dry Southwest (two tribes).

f. California Indians
g. Great Basin Indians
h. Hopi
i. Inuit
j. Iroquois
k. Mound Builders
l. Navajo
m. Plateau Indians

(12 points)

E. True or False—Chapter 2

Circle T *for* True *or* F *for* False.

T F 44. Before the Crusades, the average European knew little about sugar, spices, and other goods from the Far East.

T F 45. The Portuguese were the first Europeans to control the trade routes to the East.

T F 46. Columbus thought he could reach the East by sailing west.

T F 47. The Anabaptists promoted the idea that church and state should be separate.

T F 48. European countries had a practice that the first country to claim land in the New World could possess it.

(5 points)

F. Essay Questions—Chapters 2 and 3

49. Why does Columbus receive credit for discovering America when the Vikings had been there five hundred years earlier?

50. What were three changes other than the Reformation, which increased European interest in exploration? Along with each change, explain how it contributed to further exploration.

51. What are two contributions

   a. of the Europeans to the Indians?

   b. of the Indians to the Europeans?

52. What was one main cause of conflict between the Europeans and the Indians?

_____
_____
_____
_____

(12 points)
Total points (complete test): 60
(Chapter 2 portion): 34

Understanding North American History

Chapter 4 and 5 Test

Name _____ Date _____ Score _____

A. Matching: Terms

Not all the choices will be used.

____ 1. Tribe who sided with the English.

____ 2. "Forest runners" who gathered furs from the Indians and brought them to trading centers.

____ 3. Tribes of Indians who were baptized in large numbers; sided with the French.

____ 4. Spanish outposts intended to convert and civilize Indians.

____ 5. French Protestants.

____ 6. Form of manorialism, transplanted to New France.

____ 7. Policy in which all power is held by one person or group at the head.

____ 8. French landholders.

____ 9. Settlers who worked a seigneur's land in New France.

a. absolutism
b. coureurs de bois
c. habitants
d. Huguenots
e. Huron, Algonquin
f. Iroquois
g. Jesuits
h. missions
i. seigneurial system
j. seigneurs

(9 points)

B. Matching: Places and Dates

Not all the choices will be used.

____ 10. River along the Quebec and Montreal settlements.

____ 11. Location of Pueblo land settled by Oñate and Spanish colonists.

____ 12. Town founded by Champlain in 1608.

____ 13. Name derived from Indian word for *village*.

____ 14. Date when Florida was discovered.

____ 15. French name for the area around the Bay of Fundy.

____ 16. Poutrincourt's beloved settlement, destroyed by the English.

____ 17. Date when the Spanish Armada was defeated.

____ 18. Date when the oldest European town in the United States was founded.

____ 19. Present-day state where Eusebio Kino set up missions.

____ 20. Present-day state that was settled in the 1700s to prevent English and Russian claims.

a. Acadia
b. Arizona
c. California
d. Canada
e. New Mexico
f. Port Royal
g. Quebec
h. St. Lawrence
i. Texas
j. 1513
k. 1565
l. 1588

(11 points)

C. Completion: People

Write the correct name for each description.

_____ 21. "Father of New France."

_____ 22. Jesuits who explored part of the Mississippi (two men).
_____

_____ 23. Claimed for France the area drained by the Mississippi.

_____ 24. Early explorer who made three trips to the St. Lawrence region.

_____ 25. Explorer who sought the Seven Cities of Cíbola.

_____ 26. First explorer sent by France.

_____ 27. Man who discovered Florida while seeking the Fountain of Youth.

_____ 28. Explorer who discovered the Mississippi River.

(9 points)

D. True or False

Circle T for True or F for False.

T F 29. The Spanish respected the Indians and treated them fairly and kindly.

T F 30. The early Spanish explorers in North America were so eager to find gold that they tended to take little interest in other discoveries.

T F 31. One reason that the Spanish built missions was to protect their frontier against foreign nations.

T F 32. The Spanish operated their missions on the basis of democracy and freedom.

T F 33. Settlers in New France had freedom to own their own land, choose their own church, and set up their own government.

T F 34. The economic prosperity of New France depended on the fur trade.

T F 35. New France failed to develop rapidly.

T F 36. The French expanded into the Mississippi River valley because they wanted to farm the land.

(8 points)

E. Essay Questions

37. How was the defeat of the Spanish Armada a turning point in history?

_____

_____

_____

38. What were two effects that the Spanish had on southwestern North America?

_____

_____

_____

39. What were the duties of seigneurs in New France? of habitants?

_____

_____

_____

_____

_____

40. What were two effects that the French colonies had on North America?

_____

_____

_____

(7 points)
Total points: 44

Understanding North American History

Chapter 6 and 7 Test

Score _____

Name _____ Date _____

A. Matching: Terms

Not all the choices will be used.

____ 1. Aristocracy; upper-class people.

____ 2. Person working to repay the cost of his voyage to America.

____ 3. Colony governed by the king.

____ 4. Colony owners hoping to rent land to people of lower rank.

____ 5. Colony governed by a proprietor.

____ 6. Small farmers and craftsmen.

____ 7. Colony operating on the basis of its charter.

____ 8. Legal document granting the right to settle and govern a certain region.

____ 9. People who withdrew from the Church of England and moved to America.

____ 10. People who wanted to purify the Church of England from within.

____ 11. Maryland law granting religious freedom.

____ 12. Unskilled laborers who did not own land.

____ 13. Agreement signed by Pilgrims and Strangers to make "just and equal laws."

____ 14. Group of people appointed to make laws.

a. Act of Toleration
b. better class
c. buffer
d. charter
e. charter colony
f. indentured servant
g. legislature
h. Mayflower Compact
i. meaner sort
j. middling class
k. Pilgrims
l. proprietary colony
m. proprietors
n. Puritans
o. royal colony

(14 points)

B. Completion: Names

Write the correct name for each description.

_____ 15. Religious revival in the 1700s.

_____ 16. Noted schoolteacher in colonial Pennsylvania.

_____ 17. Quaker who received a land grant as payment for a debt.

_____ 18. Church of England; official church in the South.

_____ 19. Founder of Rhode Island, who insisted on freedom of conscience.

_____ 20. Puritan church, dominant in New England.

_____ 21. Leaders of the colonial religious revival (two men).

_____

16   Chapters 6 and 7 Test

_____ 22. Age of Reason.

_____ 23. Trustee leader in the founding of Georgia.

_____ 24. Jamestown leader who established a rule of "no work, no food."

_____ 25. Founder of Maryland.   (12 points)

C. Matching: Places and Dates

Not all the choices will be used.

____ 26. Colony intended as a haven for debtors.
____ 27. Dutch territory in America.
____ 28. Pilgrim settlement.
____ 29. City of Brotherly Love.
____ 30. Name taken from the Latin form of *Charles*.
____ 31. Roger Williams's settlement.
____ 32. Thomas Hooker's settlement.
____ 33. Puritan settlement.
____ 34. Jamestown is founded.
____ 35. Plymouth is founded.

a. Carolina
b. Connecticut
c. Georgia
d. Massachusetts Bay Colony
e. New Netherland
f. Philadelphia
g. Plymouth
h. Providence
i. 1607
j. 1620
k. 1664

(10 points)

D. True or False

Circle T *for* True *or* F *for* False.

T F 36. Maryland was founded as a haven for Quakers.

T F 37. Jamestown was settled primarily for religious freedom.

T F 38. The Carolinas were to be modeled on the manorial system.

T F 39. Pennsylvania was founded as a place of freedom for Catholics.

T F 40. The Puritans, who came for religious freedom, refused to grant full religious freedom to others.

T F 41. The Southern Colonies used the headright system.

T F 42. A triangular trade route helped to promote trade among three different American colonies.

T F 43. Colonial charters granted colonists the same privileges as Englishmen.

T F 44. The Bible had little effect on the people of early colonial days.

T F 45. Shipping and manufacturing were important in the South because of the many good harbors.

(10 points)

E. Essay Questions

46. What are two reasons that English settlers came to America?

    _____
    _____

47. Describe the founding of any two English colonies by answering two of the following questions about each. Who founded it? What were the goals? What did the colony experience as those goals were pursued?

    _____
    _____
    _____
    _____
    _____
    _____

48. What were two effects of the colonial religious revival in the 1700s?

    _____
    _____

(8 points)
Total points: 54

Understanding North American History

Chapter 8 and 9 Test

Name _____

Date _____

A. Matching: Terms and Dates

Not all the choices will be used.

____ 1. Dutch organization to help Mennonite emigrants.

____ 2. Date when first Mennonites came to America.

____ 3. Time of the Revolutionary War.

____ 4. Date when the French and Indian War began.

____ 5. Date when the French and Indian War ended.

____ 6. Pamphlet promoting independence.

____ 7. Promise to support the patriot government.

____ 8. Law that closed lands west of the Appalachians to settlement.

____ 9. Document approved on July 4, 1776.

____ 10. Persons favoring independence.

____ 11. Supporters of Great Britain.

____ 12. Parliamentary action for punishing the colonies.

____ 13. Parliamentary action for raising revenue.

____ 14. Assembly that declared independence.

____ 15. Assembly where leaders reasoned that Parliament had no authority over them.

____ 16. Agreement that ended the Revolution.

a. Coercive Acts
b. Commission for Foreign Needs
c. *Common Sense*
d. Declaration of Independence
e. First Continental Congress
f. Loyalists
g. Oath of Allegiance
h. Olive Branch Petition
i. patriots
j. Proclamation of 1763
k. Second Continental Congress
l. Stamp Act
m. Treaty of Paris
n. 1683
o. 1763
p. 1754
q. 1775–1783

(16 points)

B. Matching: People and Places

Not all the choices will be used.

___ 17. British secretary of state during French and Indian War.

___ 18. French general in the French and Indian War.

___ 19. British general defeated at Fort Duquesne.

___ 20. British general who won the battle of Quebec.

___ 21. Site of the decisive battle in the French and Indian War.

___ 22. Town in Pennsylvania where Mennonites first settled.

___ 23. Place where conflicting claims led to the French and Indian War.

___ 24. Northern feature around which the British developed fur trade.

___ 25. French fortification built where Pittsburgh now stands.

a. Braddock
b. Fort Duquesne
c. Germantown
d. Hudson Bay
e. James Wolfe
f. Montcalm
g. Ohio River valley
h. Prince Rupert
i. Quebec
j. William Pitt

(9 points)

C. Completion: People and Places

Write the correct name for each description.

_____ 26. Patriot general in command of the entire American army.

_____ 27. British general whose defeat ended the Revolution.

_____ 28. Writer of *Common Sense*.

_____ 29. Location of the battle that was the turning point in the Revolution.

_____ 30. Writer of the Declaration of Independence.

_____ 31. Meeting place of the First and Second Continental Congress.

_____ 32. King of Great Britain during the Revolution.

_____ 33. Location of the beginning battle of the Revolution (either one of two towns).

_____ 34. Location of the last major battle of the Revolution.

_____ 35. Place where the American army endured great hardship during the winter of 1777–1778.

(10 points)

D. True or False

Circle T for True or F for False.

T F 36. The French and Indian War is important in the history of North America because the French were removed as a North American power.

T F 37. Mennonites came to America to establish an ideal government.

T F 38. The Quakers refused to protect the Scotch-Irish against the Indians.

T F 39. The Americans and British disagreed about Parliament's authority over the colonies.

T F   40. The British had no right to tax the American colonies.

T F   41. The Americans believed that "taxation without representation is tyranny."

T F   42. The nonresistant groups were Tories.

(7 points)

E. Essay Questions

43. What were two issues that led to fighting between the British and the French in North America?

___

___

___

44. What did the British gain by the treaty that ended the French and Indian War?

___

___

45. a. What did the British acknowledge in the Treaty of Paris after the American Revolution?

___

___

b. What territory did the United States include at that time?

___

___

46. a. What things did the Mennonites do to maintain nonresistance before and during the French and Indian War?

___

___

___

b. What were two main issues of nonresistance during the American Revolution?

___

___

(9 points)
Total points: 51

Understanding North American History

Chapter 10 Test

Name _____   Date _____

Score _____

A. Matching: Terms

Not all the choices will be used.

___ 1. To bring to trial for misconduct in office.

___ 2. People who opposed the Constitution.

___ 3. Written plan of government.

___ 4. To reject a proposed law.

___ 5. Having a legislature with two houses.

___ 6. The act of giving formal agreement to.

___ 7. Legislative body of the United States.

___ 8. Plan with government powers divided between the states and the national government.

___ 9. Proposal calling for states to have proportionate representation.

___ 10. Law that provided a plan of government and statehood for new territories.

___ 11. Proposal calling for all states to have equal representation.

___ 12. Weak union in which states have more power than the national government.

___ 13. People who supported the Constitution.

___ 14. Dividing of government into three branches.

___ 15. Limits that government branches place on each other's powers.

___ 16. Proposal that settled the issue of representation.

a. Anti-Federalists
b. bicameral
c. checks and balances
d. confederation
e. Congress
f. constitution
g. Federalists
h. federal system
i. Great Compromise
j. impeach
k. New Jersey Plan
l. Northwest Ordinance of 1787
m. ratification
n. republic
o. separation of powers
p. veto
q. Virginia Plan

(16 points)

B. Completion: Names and Terms

Write the correct name or term for each description.

_____ 17. Branch of government that makes laws.

_____ 18. Introduction to the Constitution.

_____ 19. Branch of government that enacts laws.

_____ 20. "Father of the Constitution."

24   Chapter 10 Test

_____ 21. Branch of government that decides cases about laws.
_____ 22. Series of articles defending the Constitution.
_____ 23. Chairman of the Constitutional Convention.
_____ 24. Part of legislative branch with states represented proportionately.
_____ 25. Part of legislative branch with states represented equally.
_____ 26. Group of men who elect the president.

(10 points)

C. Dates

Give the years when the following events took place.

_____ 27. The Articles of Confederation were ratified.
_____ 28. The year of the Constitutional Convention.
_____ 29. The year when government under the Constitution began.
_____ 30. The year when the Bill of Rights was added to the Constitution.

(4 points)

D. True or False

Circle T for True or F for False.

T F 31. In the United States, the highest level of government is the national, or federal, government.

T F 32. A republic has no king and is a pure democracy.

T F 33. The Constitution prevents power from being concentrated in the hands of any one man or group of men.

T F 34. The Constitution, like the laws of the Medes and Persians, may never be changed.

T F 35. The purpose of the Bill of Rights is to guarantee freedoms to citizens of the United States.

(5 points)

E. Essay Questions

36. a. What was the main reason that government under the Articles of Confederation did not work?

_____

_____

b. What were two problems that showed the ineffectiveness of the government under the Confederation?

_____

_____

_____

_____

37. How were the following matters settled at the Constitutional Convention?

   a. The issue of representation.

   _____

   _____

   b. The issue of slavery.

   _____

   _____

38. What are two examples of checks and balances in the Constitutional government?

   _____

   _____

   _____

(7 points)
Total points: 42

Understanding North American History

Chapter 11 and 12 Test

Name _____

Score _____

Date _____

A. Matching: Terms

Not all the choices will be used.

____ 1. Favored strict interpretation and limited government.

____ 2. Boldly promoted the War of 1812.

____ 3. Ended the War of 1812.

____ 4. Settled differences with Britain.

____ 5. Pride in belonging to one's country.

____ 6. Head judge of the Supreme Court.

____ 7. Power of the Supreme Court to declare a law unconstitutional.

____ 8. Laws that restricted criticism of the government.

____ 9. Settled differences with Spain.

____ 10. Favored loose interpretation and strong government.

____ 11. Law that stopped all exports.

____ 12. Resistance to paying taxes in western Pennsylvania.

a. Alien and Sedition Acts
b. chief justice
c. Democratic-Republicans
d. Embargo Act
e. Federalists
f. impress
g. Jay Treaty
h. judicial review
i. nationalism
j. Pinckney Treaty
k. Treaty of Ghent
l. war hawks
m. Whiskey Rebellion

(12 points)

B. Matching: Terms

Not all the choices will be used.

____ 13. Idea that states are supreme over the federal government.

____ 14. To withdraw formally from an organization.

____ 15. Agreement that settled a slavery problem.

____ 16. Time of national unity and harmony.

____ 17. Political party that opposed Andrew Jackson.

____ 18. Practice in which the winner of an election rewards his supporters with government positions.

____ 19. Declaration about involvement of European and American nations in each other's affairs.

____ 20. Plan for a protective tariff, internal improvements, and a national bank.

____ 21. Agreement that gained Florida in 1819.

____ 22. Strong devotion to the interests of a local region.

a. Adams-Onís Treaty
b. American System
c. Era of Good Feelings
d. Missouri Compromise
e. Monroe Doctrine
f. nullify
g. secede
h. sectionalism
i. spoils system
j. states' rights
k. Whigs

(10 points)

C. Matching: Presidents

___ 23. First president; served from 1789 to 1797.
___ 24. First president to die in office.
___ 25. Son of a former president.
___ 26. Vice president under Andrew Jackson.
___ 27. President during War of 1812; served from 1809 to 1817.
___ 28. First vice president to fill the position of a president who died in office.
___ 29. President during the Era of Good Feelings.
___ 30. Represented the common man.
___ 31. Second president; Federalist; served from 1797 to 1801.
___ 32. Leader of Democratic-Republicans; third president; served from 1801 to 1809.

a. Andrew Jackson
b. George Washington
c. James Madison
d. James Monroe
e. John Adams
f. John Quincy Adams
g. John Tyler
h. Martin Van Buren
i. Thomas Jefferson
j. William H. Harrison

(10 points)

D. Completion: People

Write the correct name for each description.

_____ 33. Chief justice who strengthened the Supreme Court.
_____ 34. War hawks (two men).
_____
_____ 35. Tried to create an Indian confederacy.
_____ 36. Explorer for whom a mountain in Colorado is named.
_____ 37. Opened the Wilderness Road to Kentucky.
_____ 38. Federalist leader and first secretary of the treasury.
_____ 39. Explorers of the Louisiana Purchase from 1804 to 1806 (two men).
_____

(9 points)

E. True or False

Circle T for True or F for False.

T F 40. Hamilton's financial plans increased the power of the government.
T F 41. President Jefferson increased the size of the government.
T F 42. The Whig party was more like the Democratic-Republicans than like the Federalists.
T F 43. Andrew Jackson was a dignified president from an aristocratic family.

T F 44. State nullification of federal laws would have led to chaos and breakup of national unity.

T F 45. The Panic of 1837 occurred during Martin Van Buren's term as president.

T F 46. Indian removal was done to open new lands for tobacco growing.

T F 47. Andrew Jackson opposed the Bank of the United States because he believed it favored the wealthy and was unconstitutional.

T F 48. The Whigs used speeches, parades, and songs to help William Henry Harrison win election as president.

T F 49. John Tyler was a highly successful Whig president.

(10 points)

F. Essay Questions

50. a. What were two causes of the War of 1812?

_____

_____

b. What were two effects of that war?

_____

_____

_____

51. What are two of the main points in the Monroe Doctrine?

_____

_____

_____

(6 points)
Total points: 57

Understanding North American History

Chapter 13 and 14 Test

Score _____

Name _____

Date _____

A. Matching: Terms

Not all the choices will be used.

____ 1. Traveling preacher in the West.

____ 2. Waterway joining Lake Erie to the Hudson River.

____ 3. Machine for removing seeds from cotton.

____ 4. Route extending from Cumberland to Vandalia.

____ 5. Change from producing handmade goods at home to producing machine-made goods in factories.

____ 6. Region dependent on cotton.

____ 7. Large farm that produced one main crop by slave labor.

____ 8. Elimination of slavery.

____ 9. Strip of land obtained from Mexico to build a railroad.

____ 10. Independent California.

____ 11. Meeting place for fur traders to sell furs and buy supplies.

____ 12. Land gained by the Mexican War.

____ 13. Independent Texas.

____ 14. People who rushed to find gold in 1849.

____ 15. Hardy fur traders and explorers of the West.

a. abolition
b. Bear Flag Republic
c. circuit rider
d. cotton gin
e. Cotton Kingdom
f. Erie Canal
g. forty-niners
h. Gadsden Purchase
i. Industrial Revolution
j. Lone Star Republic
k. Mexican Cession
l. mountain men
m. National Road
n. plantation
o. rendezvous
p. slave code

(15 points)

B. Completion: People

Write the correct name for each description.

_____ 16. Promoter of educational reform.

_____ 17. Inventor of the telegraph.

_____ 18. Inventor of the cotton gin.

_____ 19. Brought textile manufacturing to America.

_____ 20. Designed an improved plow made of steel.

_____ 21. Built the first successful steamboat, the *Clermont*.

_____ 22. Invented the mechanical reaper.

_____ 23. "Father of American missions."

_____ 24. Published the "blue-backed speller."

_____ 25. Evangelist who used new methods to win converts.

(10 points)

C. Matching: People and Places

Not all the choices will be used.

___ 26. First president of the Lone Star Republic.

___ 27. General in the Mexican War who became president in 1848.

___ 28. Man who began colonizing Texas.

___ 29. Expansionist president who served from 1845 to 1849.

___ 30. Area of modern Oregon, Washington, and Idaho.

___ 31. Conqueror of New Mexico and California in the Mexican War.

___ 32. Missionary in Oregon who promoted settlement there.

___ 33. Fort owner on whose land gold was discovered.

___ 34. Harsh ruler and military leader of Mexico.

___ 35. Disputed boundary between Texas and Mexico.

___ 36. Conqueror of Mexico City in the Mexican War.

___ 37. Was followed by Oregon-bound travelers for hundreds of miles.

a. James K. Polk
b. James Watt
c. John Sutter
d. Marcus Whitman
e. Oregon Territory
f. Platte River
g. Rio Grande
h. Sam Houston
i. Santa Anna
j. Stephen Austin
k. Stephen Kearny
l. Winfield Scott
m. Zachary Taylor

(12 points)

D. True or False

Circle T *for* True *or* F *for* False.

T F 38. Industry grew rapidly in the North because of energy, natural resources, and transportation.

T F 39. The Erie Canal served to divert much trade away from New Orleans to New York City.

T F 40. Man's inventions and technology make people better.

T F 41. The cotton gin helped to firmly establish slavery in the South.

T F 42. Slavery helped to make the South a rich, prosperous region.

T F 43. The Bible directly condemns slavery.

T F 44. Large numbers of Americans moved to the Pacific Coast for religious reasons.

T F 45. The United States gained Texas as part of the Mexican Cession.

T F 46. Oregon was formerly shared with the British.

T F 47. The Mexican War contributed to the Civil War.

(10 points)

E. Essay Questions

48. What are two changes that the Industrial Revolution brought to America?

49. What are two lasting effects that the Second Great Awakening had on the United States?

50. What was manifest destiny, and how was it expressed?

51. What was one cause and one effect of the Mexican War?

52. Choose one of the following things, and write some specific details about it.

   the pony express

   traveling on the Oregon Trail

   the life of the miner during the California gold rush

(10 points)
Total points: 57

Understanding North American History

Chapter 15 and 16 Test

Name _____ Date _____

Score _____

A. Matching: Terms

Not all the choices will be used.

____ 1. Statement declaring that slaves in the Confederacy were free.

____ 2. Confederate soldiers.

____ 3. Agreement that let California become a free state.

____ 4. Measure that permanently outlawed slavery.

____ 5. Idea that people living in an area should decide for themselves about slavery.

____ 6. Delaware, Maryland, Kentucky, and Missouri.

____ 7. Northern soldiers.

____ 8. Payment to avoid military service.

____ 9. Secret system that aided slaves in escaping.

____ 10. Ship that changed naval warfare.

a. border states
b. commutation fee
c. Compromise of 1850
d. Emancipation Proclamation
e. Fugitive Slave Law
f. ironclad
g. popular sovereignty
h. "Rebels"
i. Thirteenth Amendment
j. Underground Railroad
k. "Yankees"

(10 points)

B. Completion: People

Write the correct name for each description.

_____ 11. President of the Confederate States of America.

_____ 12. "President of the Underground Railroad."

_____ 13. Union president during the Civil War.

_____ 14. Black man who was denied freedom by the Supreme Court.

_____ 15. Union president who did little about Southern secession.

_____ 16. Man who promoted popular sovereignty and debated with Lincoln.

_____ 17. Author of *Uncle Tom's Cabin*.

_____ 18. Man who tried to free the slaves through an armed uprising.

_____ 19. Chief Union general at the end of the Civil War.

_____ 20. Union general who devastated the Shenandoah Valley.

_____ 21. Union general who led the destructive March to the Sea.

36 Chapters 15 and 16 Test

_____ 22. Chief general of the Confederate armies.

_____ 23. Confederate general shot by his own men at Chancellorsville.

_____ 24. Union naval commander who took New Orleans and Mobile.

(14 points)

C. Matching: Places

Not all the choices will be used.

____ 25. Town where the Confederacy reached its "high-water mark."

____ 26. Place where the Civil War began.

____ 27. Confederate capital.

____ 28. Stronghold whose fall allowed Union control of the Mississippi.

____ 29. Battle that gave Lincoln an occasion to issue the Emancipation Proclamation.

____ 30. New state formed during the Civil War.

____ 31. Early battle that showed the war would be long and hard.

a. Antietam
b. First Battle of Bull Run
c. Chancellorsville
d. Fort Sumter
e. Gettysburg
f. Richmond
g. Vicksburg
h. West Virginia

(7 points)

D. True or False

Circle T for True or F for False.

T F 32. Southern states began to secede from the Union after Lincoln was elected in 1860.

T F 33. The Civil War began as a war to free the slaves.

T F 34. The South hoped to win the war by crushing the North.

T F 35. The Civil War lasted from 1861 to 1865.

T F 36. Lincoln's assassination was a great loss to both the North and the South.

(5 points)

E. Essay Questions

37. a. How did slavery relate to states' rights?

_____

_____

b. How did slavery relate to control of the federal government?

_____

_____

38. How did each side hope to win the Civil War?

_____

_____

_____

39. What were two important results of the Civil War?

_____

_____

_____

40. What was one difficulty that nonresistant people faced in the North? in the South?

_____

_____

_____

(8 points)
Total points: 44

Understanding North American History

Chapter 17 Test

Name _____ Date _____ Score _____

A. Matching: Terms

Not all the choices will be used.

____ 1. Government agency that aided the South after the Civil War.

____ 2. President Lincoln's plan for Reconstruction.

____ 3. Northerners who went south to help in Reconstruction.

____ 4. System in which farm workers rent cropland and use a share of the crops to pay the rent.

____ 5. Measure that granted citizenship to blacks.

____ 6. Rebuilding and restoration of the South after the Civil War.

____ 7. Former slaves.

____ 8. Secret society that terrorized blacks.

____ 9. Social separation based on race.

____ 10. Southern whites who took part in Reconstruction governments.

____ 11. Group that wanted to punish and reform the South.

____ 12. Dependable Southern support of the Democratic Party.

____ 13. To restore government control by whites to a Southern state.

____ 14. Measure granting all citizens the right to vote.

____ 15. Measure that provided military control to enforce Reconstruction.

____ 16. Laws that restricted blacks.

a. Amnesty Act
b. black codes
c. carpetbaggers
d. Fifteenth Amendment
e. Fourteenth Amendment
f. freedmen
g. Freedmen's Bureau
h. Ku Klux Klan
i. Radical Republicans
j. Reconstruction
k. Reconstruction Act
l. redeem
m. scalawags
n. segregation
o. sharecropping
p. solid South
q. ten percent plan

(16 points)

B. Completion: People and Places

Write the correct name for each description.

_____ 17. President who was impeached in 1868.

_____ 18. Former Civil War general who became president.

_____ 19. "Seward's Folly."

_____ 20. President appointed after disputed election and the Compromise of 1877.

_____ 21. Black leader who founded the Tuskegee Institute.

_____ 22. Johnson's secretary of state who purchased a new territory.

_____ 23. Black scientist who encouraged raising peanuts in the South.

(7 points)

C. True or False

Circle T *for* True *or* F *for* False.

T F 24. The Radicals wanted to make blacks and whites equal by law.

T F 25. Southern states established black codes to aid the blacks' adjustment to freedom.

T F 26. President Johnson was impeached because he had done something unconstitutional.

T F 27. Redeemed governments tried to undo the accomplishments of the Reconstruction governments.

(4 points)

D. Essay Questions

28. What are two reasons that Reconstruction was necessary?

29. a. What was one accomplishment of the Reconstruction governments?

   b. What was one of their problems?

30. What were two difficulties that blacks faced during and after Reconstruction?

(6 points)
Total points: 33

Understanding North American History

Chapter 18 Test

Score _____

Name _____

Date _____

A. Matching: Terms

Not all the choices will be used.

____ 1. Union of provinces under a single government.

____ 2. Strong French-Canadian canoe paddlers.

____ 3. Métis uprising that led to the establishment of Manitoba.

____ 4. Rule by a small group of people.

____ 5. Nobleman's proposal for changes in Canadian government.

____ 6. Law that joined two provinces into the Province of Canada.

____ 7. Meeting where Confederation was planned.

____ 8. Men sent to stop the whiskey trade and to deal with the Indians.

____ 9. Left the United States to remain under British rule.

____ 10. Trade agreement with the United States.

____ 11. Law that created the Dominion of Canada.

____ 12. Government controlled by the people rather than by aristocrats.

____ 13. Small group of wealthy men who controlled Canadian government.

____ 14. Program that included tariffs, railroad construction, and settlement of the Northwest.

a. Act of Union
b. British North America Act
c. confederation
d. Durham Report
e. Family Compact
f. National Policy
g. North West Mounted Police
h. oligarchy
i. Quebec Conference
j. Rebellion of 1837
k. Reciprocity Treaty
l. Red River Rebellion
m. responsible government
n. United Empire Loyalists
o. voyageurs

(14 points)

B. Completion: Names

Write the correct name for each description.

_____ 15. First prime minister of Canada.

_____ 16. Métis leader of rebellions.

_____ 17. Reached the Pacific by land in trying to find the Northwest Passage.

_____ 18. Governor of British Columbia who built the Cariboo Road.

_____ 19. Famous surveyor who explored the Columbia River.

42 Chapter 18 Test

_____ 20. Legislature of the Dominion, including Senate and House of Commons.

_____ 21. Produced a report that led to changes in Canadian government.

_____ 22. Canadian colonel in the War of 1812.

(8 points)

C. True or False

Circle T *for* True *or* F *for* False.

T F 23. The oligarchy of Upper Canada opposed responsible government.

T F 24. The French people were eager to modernize Lower Canada by adopting English ways.

T F 25. The Fraser River gold rush had more law and order than the California gold rush did.

T F 26. The Canadian Parliament created the Dominion of Canada.

T F 27. The Dominion of Canada became a nation on July 1, 1867.

T F 28. The first prime minister of the Dominion of Canada promoted a transcontinental railroad to link the provinces together.

T F 29. The four provinces that formed the Dominion of Canada were Ontario, Quebec, New Brunswick, and Newfoundland.

(7 points)

D. Essay Questions

30. What are two ways that the War of 1812 affected Canada?

_____

_____

_____

31. What were two factors that led Canada to become a Confederation?

_____

_____

_____

32. How was British Columbia persuaded to join the Dominion of Canada rather than to join the United States?

_____

_____

(5 points)
Total points: 34

Understanding North American History

Chapter 19 Test

Name _____   Date _____

A. Matching: People and Places

Not all the choices will be used.

____ 1. Invented barbed wire in 1874.

____ 2. Lost the Battle of the Little Bighorn.

____ 3. Built stockyards at Abilene, Kansas.

____ 4. Last great Apache leader, who surrendered in 1886.

____ 5. Indian leader whose people were massacred at Sand Creek.

____ 6. Rich gold and silver strike in Nevada.

____ 7. Man who invented the air brake for trains in 1869.

____ 8. Nez Perce leader who went on a long flight with his people before capture.

____ 9. Indian chiefs at the Battle of the Little Bighorn (two answers).

____ 10. Route of cattle herds moving north to Kansas.

____ 11. Place where the transcontinental railroad was joined.

____ 12. One of the first cattle ranchers in Texas.

____ 13. Place where last Indian war took place.

a. Black Kettle
b. Charles Goodnight
c. Chief Joseph
d. Chisholm Trail
e. Comstock Lode
f. Crazy Horse
g. George Custer
h. George Westinghouse
i. Geronimo
j. Joseph Glidden
k. Joseph McCoy
l. Pikes Peak
m. Promontory
n. Sitting Bull
o. Wounded Knee

(14 points)

B. Matching: Terms

Not all the choices will be used.

____ 14. Built railroad west from Nebraska.

____ 15. Belief in return of Indians and buffalo.

____ 16. Law that divided reservations into family farms.

____ 17. Built railroad east from California.

____ 18. Taking of cattle over a trail to cattle towns.

____ 19. Law that authorized a transcontinental railroad.

____ 20. Law that allowed settlers to claim 160 acres (65 ha) of land for farming.

a. Central Pacific
b. Dawes Act
c. Ghost Dance religion
d. Homestead Act
e. Indian Reorganization Act
f. "long drive"
g. Pacific Railroad Act
h. Union Pacific

(7 points)

C. Completion: Terms

Write the correct term for each description.

_____ 21. Main vein of ore.

_____ 22. Person who claimed land and settled on it for five years.

_____ 23. Land owned by the government.

_____ 24. Group that meted out swift and stern justice.

_____ 25. Unfenced grazing land.

(5 points)

D. True or False

Circle T for True or F for False.

T F 26. When prospectors found gold, they often used their wealth to establish a gold mining corporation.

T F 27. The miners exemplified the American tendency to govern themselves in the absence of established government.

T F 28. Greed was a chief cause of the Indian wars.

T F 29. The cattle kingdom had little to do with transportation.

T F 30. The Homestead Act encouraged settlement of the West by providing cheap or free land.

(5 points)

E. Essay Questions

31. Both miners and railroads contributed to settling the West.

    a. How did miners help?

    _____

    _____

    b. How did railroads help?

    _____

    _____

32. What were two main causes of the Indian wars?

    _____

    _____

    _____

33. Give two answers to each question.

   a. What were some major difficulties that homesteaders experienced?

   _____

   _____

   _____

   b. How did they overcome those difficulties?

   _____

   _____

   _____

(8 points)
Total points: 39

Understanding North American History

Chapter 20 Test

Score _____

Name _____

Date _____

A. Matching: People and Terms

Not all the choices will be used.

____ 1. Evangelist who introduced revival meetings into the Mennonite Church.

____ 2. Reformer who founded the Hull House in Chicago.

____ 3. Inventor of the telephone.

____ 4. Inventor of the electric light bulb.

____ 5. Man whose company helped make the United States a leading steel producer.

____ 6. Famous evangelist in the latter half of the 1800s.

____ 7. Presidential candidate in 1896 who supported free silver.

____ 8. Scientist who developed new varieties of plants.

____ 9. Group that checked the qualifications of prospective government employees.

____ 10. Man who developed the Standard Oil corporation.

____ 11. Measure that established an agency to regulate railroads.

____ 12. Group that developed from Farmers' Alliances and promoted radical changes.

____ 13. Measure allowing the government to attack businesses that it considered monopolies.

____ 14. Theory that living things had a natural origin and that they gradually evolved into the species existing today.

a. Alexander Graham Bell
b. Andrew Carnegie
c. Civil Service Commission
d. Darwinism
e. Dwight L. Moody
f. Interstate Commerce Act
g. Jane Addams
h. John D. Rockefeller
i. John S. Coffman
j. Luther Burbank
k. Populist Party
l. Republican Party
m. Sherman Antitrust Act
n. Thomas Alva Edison
o. William Jennings Bryan

(14 points)

B. Matching: Presidents

___ 15. Served two nonconsecutive terms.
___ 16. Took office in 1881 when the previous president was assassinated.
___ 17. Served at the time of the "Billion Dollar Congress."
___ 18. Came into office through a disputed election.
___ 19. Supported the gold standard and conducted a "front-porch" campaign.
___ 20. Served only a few months before being assassinated.

a. Rutherford B. Hayes
b. James A. Garfield
c. Chester A. Arthur
d. Grover Cleveland
e. Benjamin Harrison
f. William McKinley

(6 points)

C. Completion: Terms

Write the correct term for each description.

_____ 21. System including free markets and private ownership of property.
_____ 22. Large business owned by many people.
_____ 23. Scarce product + great demand = high price; abundant product + low demand = low price.
_____ 24. System for making large numbers of products by using interchangeable parts and assembly lines.
_____ 25. Organized group controlled by a powerful "boss."
_____ 26. Movement to limit immigration.
_____ 27. Religious movement designed to improve social conditions.
_____ 28. Place where people of many different nationalities mingle together.
_____ 29. Karl Marx's theory proposing a classless society and government ownership of businesses.
_____ 30. Religious movement emphasizing conversion more than discipleship.

(10 points)

D. True or False

Circle T for True or F for False.

T F 31. Labor unions are inconsistent with the Bible doctrine of nonresistance and a Scriptural approach to working.

T F 32. Darwin's theory of evolution had wide influence.

T F 33. A cooperative is a company that has no competition because it controls a certain market.

T F 34. Immigrants made only a few contributions to the United States.

T F 35. American farmers suffered hardships because they were so successful.

T F 36. Regulation of big business corporations decreased in the 1890s.

(6 points)

E. Essay Questions

37. What is one way that the United States benefited from the many immigrants who came?

38. What was one reason that cities grew so rapidly in the latter 1800s?

39. How did promoters of the social gospel try to make reforms?

40. What was one change that the Mennonite Church experienced by 1900?

(4 points)
Total points: 40

Understanding North American History

Chapter 21 and 22 Test

Score _____

Name _____

Date _____

A. Matching: Terms

Not all the choices will be used.

____ 1. Crusade that promoted reform and change.

____ 2. Law that reduced import taxes and provided for an income tax.

____ 3. Basis for American relations with countries in the Far East.

____ 4. Area in China in which a foreign nation controlled the trade and port cities.

____ 5. Policy of gaining control over foreign territory.

____ 6. Established a central banking system in 1913.

____ 7. Theodore Roosevelt's reform program to treat everyone equally.

____ 8. Policy of having little to do with foreign nations.

____ 9. Policy of United States intervention in Latin America.

____ 10. Woodrow Wilson's reform program to restore competition in business.

____ 11. Uprising in China in 1900.

____ 12. New political group that started in 1912.

a. Boxer Rebellion
b. Federal Reserve Act
c. imperialism
d. isolationism
e. muckraker
f. New Freedom
g. Open Door Policy
h. progressive movement
i. Progressive Party
j. Roosevelt Corollary
k. sphere of influence
l. Square Deal
m. Underwood Tariff Act

(12 points)

B. Matching: Places and Dates

Not all the choices will be used.

____ 13. Spanish islands in the Far East conquered by the United States and purchased for $20 million.

____ 14. Pacific islands lying about 2,000 miles west of the United States; annexed in 1898.

____ 15. Spanish island in the Caribbean that was ceded to the United States in 1898.

____ 16. Spanish island in the Pacific that was ceded to the United States in 1898.

____ 17. Island in the Caribbean that the United States conquered and gave independence in 1902.

____ 18. Year the Boxer Rebellion broke out.

____ 19. Year the Spanish-American War was fought.

____ 20. Year when Hawaii became a state of the United States.

a. Cuba
b. Guam
c. Hawaii
d. Philippines
e. Puerto Rico
f. Samoa
g. 1898
h. 1900
i. 1934
j. 1959

(8 points)

C. Matching: People and Amendments

Choices may be used twice or not at all.

___ 21. Amendment that allowed women to vote.

___ 22. Amendment that provided for the direct election of senators.

___ 23. Amendment that prohibited alcoholic beverages.

___ 24. Amendment that allowed an income tax.

___ 25. President during the Spanish-American War.

___ 26. Secretary of state who dealt with China and Panama.

___ 27. President who used "dollar diplomacy" in Latin America.

___ 28. President of the Square Deal and the "big stick."

___ 29. Democrat who was elected president after a split in the opposing party.

___ 30. President who later became a justice of the Supreme Court.

___ 31. President who promoted the New Freedom program.

a. John Dewey
b. John Hay
c. Theodore Roosevelt
d. William Gorgas
e. William Howard Taft
f. William McKinley
g. Woodrow Wilson
h. Sixteenth Amendment
i. Seventeenth Amendment
j. Eighteenth Amendment
k. Nineteenth Amendment

(11 points)

D. True or False

Circle T for True or F for False.

T F 32. The imperialism of the 1890s marked a major shift from the isolationism of the previous thirty years.

T F 33. The United States had no interest in foreign territories before the 1890s.

T F 34. The Open Door Policy marked a bold advance in United States involvement in world affairs.

T F 35. The Open Door Policy was designed to let various foreign nations divide China among themselves.

T F 36. Latin American countries welcomed United States intervention to solve their problems.

T F 37. The United States actively tried to help the territories it had conquered.

T F 38. Progressive reformers believed that social problems resulted from man's sinful condition.

T F 39. Progressive educators changed the schools to be more traditional.

T F 40. Progressive reform usually began at the federal level and then moved down to states and cities.

T F 41. Theodore Roosevelt promoted government involvement in conservation of natural resources.

(10 points)

E. Essay Questions

42. What were two effects of the Spanish-American War?

43. Why did the United States need the Panama Canal?

44. a. Who were the progressive reformers?

   b. What two reforms did they want to make in the government?

   c. What two reforms did they want to make in society?

(8 points)
Total points: 49

Understanding North American History

Chapter 23 Test

Name _____

Score _____

Date _____

A. Matching: Terms

Not all the choices will be used.

____ 1. United States army sent to France.

____ 2. Woodrow Wilson's ideas for peace.

____ 3. Organization to maintain world peace.

____ 4. Russia, France, Great Britain, and Italy.

____ 5. Right of any merchant ship to sail the ocean in peace or war.

____ 6. Agreement that punished Germany harshly and proposed an international organization for world peace.

____ 7. Items sold to help pay for the war.

____ 8. Germany, Austria-Hungary, Bulgaria, and Turkey.

____ 9. Law providing for a military draft.

a. Allies
b. American Expeditionary Force
c. Central Powers
d. Fourteen Points
e. freedom of the seas
f. League of Nations
g. Liberty Bonds
h. noncombatant
i. Selective Service Act
j. Treaty of Versailles

(9 points)

B. Completion: People, Places, Dates

Write the correct name or date for each description.

_____ 10. Year when World War I began.

_____ 11. Year when the United States entered World War I.

_____ 12. Year when World War I ended.

_____ 13. United States president during World War I.

_____ 14. General of the American army in France.

_____ 15. Place where Germany signed the peace treaty.

(6 points)

C. True or False

Circle T for True or F for False.

T F 16. World War I was the first war in which American soldiers fought in Europe.

T F 17. At the peace conference in Paris, Woodrow Wilson wanted to harshly punish Germany while the other Allied leaders wanted to be more lenient.

T F 18. If all nations would unite, there would be no more war.

T F 19. World War I led to World War II.

T F 20. World War I prompted Mennonites to become more active in relief work, to provide a better alternative for conscientious objectors in future wars, and to produce more literature to give clear teaching on nonresistance.

(5 points)

D. Essay Questions

21. a. What was the spark that ignited the Great War in Europe?

    b. What happened along the Western Front for over three years?

22. a. What was one reason that the United States began favoring the Allies in the Great War?

    b. What was one specific issue that brought the United States into the war?

23. How did the Treaty of Versailles meet the goals of both the American president and the leaders of the Allied nations in Europe?

24. What are two ways in which World War I brought suffering to nonresistant people?

(8 points)
Total points: 28

Understanding North American History

Chapter 24 Test

Name _____ Date _____

Score _____

A. Matching: People
Not all the choices will be used.

____ 1. Was elected president in 1932; introduced the New Deal.

____ 2. Took office after the death of the previous president; served from 1923 to 1929.

____ 3. Was president when the Great Depression began; served from 1929 to 1933.

____ 4. Was president from 1921 to 1923; died in office.

____ 5. Made the first solo flight across the Atlantic Ocean in 1927.

____ 6. Made cars available to the masses by introducing the Model T.

____ 7. Made the first successful flight with a heavier-than-air machine in 1903.

____ 8. Served as director of the Federal Bureau of Investigation.

a. Calvin Coolidge
b. Charles Lindbergh
c. Franklin D. Roosevelt
d. George R. Brunk
e. Henry Ford
f. Herbert Hoover
g. J. Edgar Hoover
h. Warren G. Harding
i. Wright brothers

(8 points)

B. Matching: Agencies and Programs
Not all the choices will be used.

a. Federal Bureau of Investigation
b. Federal Deposit Insurance Corporation
c. Federal Emergency Relief Administration
d. Federal Insurance Contributions Act
e. National Recovery Administration
f. Rural Electrification Administration
g. Securities and Exchange Commission
h. Tennessee Valley Authority

____ 9. Provided money for retired workers and for unemployment compensation, aid to children, and public health programs.

____ 10. Enforced federal laws.

____ 11. Provided dams to control flooding and produce electricity.

____ 12. Prevented illegal and unsound practices in the stock market.

____ 13. Brought electricity to farms and homes in the country.

____ 14. Insured bank deposits.

(6 points)

C. Completion: Terms

Write the correct term for each description.

_____ 15. Set of beliefs including the theory of evolution, rejection of the supernatural, and acceptance of science as the only source of truth.

_____ 16. Region of severe drought in the 1930s.

_____ 17. Periodic swing between prosperity and decline in the economy.

_____ 18. Event in 1925 when fundamentalists and modernists clashed over evolution.

_____ 19. Person finishing a term after another is elected to replace him.

_____ 20. Group of government programs designed to end the economic downturn in the 1930s.

_____ 21. Period when alcoholic drinks were outlawed.

_____ 22. Movement to assert basic truths of the Bible and oppose modernism.

_____ 23. Long economic downturn from 1929 to 1939.

(9 points)

D. True or False

Circle T for True or F for False.

T F 24. The Republican presidents of the 1920s increased government regulation of business.

T F 25. Most farmers prospered in the 1920s.

T F 26. Prohibition failed because laws and social pressure cannot reform man's sinful nature.

T F 27. The only thing President Hoover did about the Depression was to encourage people to help themselves.

T F 28. The New Deal helped to shorten the Depression.

(5 points)

E. Essay Questions

29. What are two ways in which the automobile changed American life?

_____
_____
_____
_____

30. What were two basic points that fundamentalism emphasized?

_____
_____
_____

31. What were two effects of the Great Depression?

_____
_____
_____

32. What were two long-term effects of the New Deal?

_____
_____
_____
_____

(8 points)
Total points: 36

Understanding North American History

Chapter 25 Test

Score _____

Name _____

Date _____

A. Matching: Terms 1

Not all the choices will be used.

____ 1. Germany and the nations that helped it in World War II.

____ 2. Political system of nationalism and totalitarian control in Germany.

____ 3. Barrier to communication and travel between communist nations and free nations.

____ 4. Hitler's destruction of millions of Jews and others in Europe.

____ 5. Having a single authority with absolute control of everything.

____ 6. Policy of maintaining peace by letting an aggressor have his way.

____ 7. Great Britain, the United States, and the nations that helped them.

____ 8. Political system of totalitarian control in Italy.

a. Allies
b. appeasement
c. Axis
d. communism
e. fascism
f. Holocaust
g. Iron Curtain
h. Nazism
i. totalitarian

(8 points)

B. Matching: Terms 2

Not all the choices will be used.

____ 9. Nations not aligned with the United States or the Soviet Union.

____ 10. International organization to maintain world peace.

____ 11. Program to build the atomic bomb.

____ 12. Program of alternate service for conscientious objectors.

____ 13. Military alliance formed by Western nations in 1949 to oppose communism.

____ 14. Conflict in which enemy nations worked against each other without actually fighting.

____ 15. Military alliance formed by communist nations of Eastern Europe in 1955.

____ 16. Body of the United Nations responsible for keeping peace.

a. Civilian Public Service
b. Cold War
c. General Assembly
d. Manhattan Project
e. North Atlantic Treaty Organization
f. Security Council
g. Third World
h. United Nations
i. Warsaw Pact

(8 points)

C. Completion: People and Dates

Write the correct name or date for each description.

_____ 17. Dictator of the Soviet Union.

_____ 18. Supreme commander of Allied forces in Europe.

_____ 19. United States president during most of World War II; first president to serve more than two terms.

_____ 20. President who replaced Roosevelt and ordered use of the atomic bomb.

_____ 21. Dictator of Germany.

_____ 22. Dictator of Italy.

_____ 23. Prime minister of Great Britain during World War II.

_____ 24. American general who helped to liberate the Philippines.

_____ 25. Year when World War II began.

_____ 26. Year when the United States entered World War II.

_____ 27. Year when World War II ended.

_____ 28. Place attacked by the Japanese on the "date of infamy."

_____ 29. Japanese city devastated by an atomic bomb in 1945.

_____ 30. Part of Germany with a Communist government after the war.

(14 points)

D. True or False

Circle T for True or F for False.

T F 31. Hitler believed that Germans were a superior race and that Jews were inferior.

T F 32. In World War II, the Soviet Union was first an ally and later an enemy of Germany.

T F 33. The Americans engaged in an island-hopping campaign against Germany.

T F 34. The Mennonite Church did little to make things easier for conscientious objectors in World War II.

(4 points)

E. Essay Questions

Give at least two answers for each question.

35. What were some ways that World War II affected the American people?

_____

_____

36. a. What were some costs of World War II?

_____
_____
_____

b. What were some major consequences of the war?

_____
_____

37. a. What kinds of work did conscientious objectors do in Civilian Public Service?

_____
_____
_____

b. What difficulties did they face?

_____
_____

(10 points)
Total points: 44

Understanding North American History

Chapter 26 and 27 Test

Name _____

Score _____

Date _____

A. Matching: Terms and Dates

Not all the choices will be used.

____ 1. Idea that if one nation in a region falls to communism, nearby nations will also fall.

____ 2. Drive to give blacks equal status with whites.

____ 3. Measure that lowered the voting age to eighteen.

____ 4. Measure that gave President Johnson power to use military force in Vietnam.

____ 5. President Truman's program of social reforms.

____ 6. Case in which separate but equal facilities for blacks were declared unconstitutional.

____ 7. Measure limiting a president's administration to two terms.

____ 8. Program for conscientious objectors from the 1950s to the 1970s.

____ 9. Title of President Johnson's social programs.

____ 10. Ending of separation by race.

____ 11. Incident in which Soviet weapons threatened United States security.

____ 12. Youth who rebelled against established values and violated social customs.

____ 13. Name of Kennedy's domestic program.

____ 14. Years of the Korean War.

____ 15. Year when the United States withdrew from Vietnam.

a. *Brown v. Board of Education of Topeka*
b. civil rights movement
c. counterculture
d. Cuban missile crisis
e. desegregation
f. domino theory
g. Fair Deal
h. Great Society
i. I-W service
j. New Frontier
k. Tonkin Gulf Resolution
l. Twenty-second Amendment
m. Twenty-fifth Amendment
n. Twenty-sixth Amendment
o. Viet Cong
p. 1950–1953
q. 1964–1973
r. 1968
s. 1973

(15 points)

B. Completion: People and Places

Write the correct name for each description.

_____ 16. General in the Korean War who was dismissed by President Truman.

_____ 17. Black minister who led the civil rights movement and promoted non-violent resistance.

_____ 18. President who served from 1945 to 1953, after Franklin D. Roosevelt.

_____ 19. President during most of the 1950s; served from 1953 to 1961.

_____ 20. Vice president who succeeded John Kennedy as president in 1963 and was re-elected in 1964.

_____ 21. President elected in 1960 and assassinated in 1963.

_____ 22. President when United States troops were withdrawn from Vietnam.

_____ 23. One of two new states added to the Union in 1959.

_____ 24. Nation that was invaded by its communist neighbor in 1950.

_____ 25. Non-communist land supported by the United States in the Vietnam War.

_____ 26. First American astronaut to orbit the earth.

(11 points)

C. True or False

Circle T for True or F for False.

T F 27. The Supreme Court became more activist in the 1950s and 1960s.

T F 28. The first space satellite was *Explorer 1*, which the United States launched in 1957.

T F 29. President Truman limited the war in Korea for fear that World War III might break out.

T F 30. The Cold War eased somewhat in the middle 1950s.

T F 31. The Cuban missile crisis was resolved when the United States invaded Cuba and destroyed the missiles.

T F 32. The New Frontier was Kennedy's program for federal aid to education, medical care for the elderly, urban renewal, and help for the poor.

T F 33. The Great Society increased government spending on welfare programs and encouraged people to receive welfare instead of working.

T F 34. Supreme Court decisions in the 1960s allowed Bible reading and prayer in public schools.

(8 points)

D. Essay Questions

35. What were two effects of the Korean War?

_____

_____

_____

36. What were two results of the Vietnam War?

_____

_____

_____

_____

37. What were some social changes among blacks in the 1960s? among youth? among women? Describe at least one for each group.

_____

_____

_____

38. a. What was one kind of work that young men did in the I-W program?

_____

_____

   b. Name two spiritual dangers that they faced.

_____

_____

_____

(10 points)
Total points: 44

Understanding North American History

Chapter 28 Test

Name _____   Date _____

A. Matching: Terms and Dates

Not all the choices will be used.

____ 1. Year of the Persian Gulf War.

____ 2. Program for restoring the economy in the 1980s.

____ 3. United States bicentennial year.

____ 4. Rising prices along with business decline in the 1970s.

____ 5. Effort in which Iraqis were driven out of Kuwait.

____ 6. Arms reduction agreement made with the Soviet Union in 1972.

____ 7. Incident when Americans were held captive in Tehran.

____ 8. Relaxing of tension between rivals.

____ 9. Measure stating that Congress could not raise its pay until after an election; ratified in 1992.

____ 10. Government agency established in 1970 to limit pollution.

____ 11. Removal of government controls.

____ 12. Scandal that led to the resignation of a president.

____ 13. One who uses violence and threats to intimidate people, especially for political purposes.

____ 14. Incident when profits from the sale of weapons were used to help fighters in Nicaragua.

a. deregulation
b. détente
c. Environmental Protection Agency
d. Iran-Contra affair
e. Iran hostage crisis
f. North American Free Trade Agreement
g. Persian Gulf War
h. "Reaganomics"
i. SALT I
j. stagflation
k. terrorist
l. Twenty-seventh Amendment
m. Watergate
n. 1976
o. 1979
p. 1991

(14 points)

B. Completion: People and Places

Write the correct name for each description.

_____ 15. First woman appointed to the Supreme Court.

_____ 16. First man to walk on the moon.

_____ 17. First unelected president; took office when the previous president resigned; served from 1974 to 1977.

_____ 18. First president to be born after World War II; served from 1993 to 2001; was impeached.

_____ 19. First president to resign from office; served from 1969 to 1974.

_____ 20. President who brought economic recovery; served from 1981 to 1989.

70 Chapter 28 Test

_____ 21. President when the Cold War ended and the Persian Gulf War was fought; served from 1989 to 1993.

_____ 22. President who faced economic troubles and the Iran hostage crisis; served from 1977 to 1981.

_____ 23. Nation of Central America that the United States invaded in 1989 to remove a corrupt dictator from office.

_____ 24. Caribbean island invaded by American troops in 1983 to keep it from becoming communist.

_____ 25. Large communist nation that dissolved in 1991.   (11 points)

C. True or False

Circle T *for* True *or* F *for* False.

T F 26. The United States was plagued with economic problems in the 1970s.

T F 27. An economic expansion began in the middle 1980s.

T F 28. The Cold War ended when Communist governments of Eastern Europe fell during 1979 and 1980.

T F 29. In the 1990s, the United States tended to intervene in the affairs of other nations for humanitarian reasons.

T F 30. One reason for social decay is the failure of many churches to uphold the truth.

T F 31. Ronald Reagan's appointments to the Supreme Court made it more liberal and activist.

(6 points)

D. Essay Questions

32. For what wrongdoing did President Nixon resign from office in 1974?

_____

_____

33. What were two things that President Reagan did to improve the economy?

_____

_____

_____

34. What were two events that brought the Cold War to an end?

_____

_____

_____

(5 points)
Total points: 36

Understanding North American History

Final Test

Name _____

Score _____

Date _____

Each set of matching exercises has at least one choice that will not be used.

A. Matching: Terms
Part 1

____ 1. Colony owners.

____ 2. Persons who withdrew from the Church of England and moved to America.

____ 3. Persons favoring independence from Britain in the Revolution.

____ 4. Supporters of Great Britain in the Revolution.

____ 5. Agreement that ended the American Revolution.

____ 6. Modified form of manorialism, transplanted to New France.

____ 7. System in which a lord owned land and serfs farmed it for him.

____ 8. Religious revival in the 1700s.

____ 9. Legal document granting rights to settle an area and to establish a government there.

____ 10. Agreement signed by Pilgrims and Strangers to make "just and equal laws."

a. charter
b. Great Awakening
c. Loyalists
d. manorialism
e. Mayflower Compact
f. patriots
g. Pilgrims
h. proprietors
i. Puritans
j. seigneurial system
k. Treaty of Paris

Part 2

____ 11. Branch of government that decides cases about laws.

____ 12. Political party that favored strict interpretation and limited government.

____ 13. First ten amendments to the Constitution, added in 1791.

____ 14. Political party that favored loose interpretation and strong government.

____ 15. Limits that government branches place on each other's powers.

____ 16. Written plan of government.

____ 17. Branch of government that enacts and enforces laws.

____ 18. Dividing of government into three branches.

____ 19. Branch of government that makes laws.

____ 20. Part of legislative branch with states represented proportionately.

a. Bill of Rights
b. checks and balances
c. constitution
d. Democratic-Republicans
e. executive
f. Federalists
g. House
h. judicial
i. legislative
j. Senate
k. separation of powers

Part 3

a. abolition
b. black codes
c. carpetbaggers
d. Emancipation Proclamation
e. Era of Good Feelings
f. freedmen
g. Industrial Revolution
h. manifest destiny
i. Missouri Compromise
j. Monroe Doctrine
k. popular sovereignty
l. Reconstruction
m. sectionalism
n. segregation
o. sharecropping
p. spoils system
q. states' rights

____ 21. Social separation based on race.

____ 22. Idea that the United States was intended to spread over the whole North American continent.

____ 23. Elimination of slavery.

____ 24. Change from producing handmade goods at home to producing machine-made goods in factories.

____ 25. Declaration about involvement of European and American nations in each other's affairs.

____ 26. Idea that people living in an area should decide for themselves about slavery.

____ 27. Measure which declared that slaves in the Confederacy were free.

____ 28. Northerners who took part in Reconstruction governments.

____ 29. Strong devotion to the interests of a local region.

____ 30. Time of national unity and harmony with only one political party.

____ 31. Idea that states are supreme over the federal government.

____ 32. Practice of replacing former officeholders with supporters.

____ 33. Agreement that settled a slavery problem in 1820.

____ 34. Laws that restricted blacks after the Civil War.

____ 35. System in which farm workers rent cropland and use a share of the crops to pay the rent.

Part 4

a. Civilian Public Service
b. Darwinism
c. free enterprise
d. Great Depression
e. imperialism
f. isolationism
g. League of Nations
h. mass production
i. New Deal
j. "new immigration"
k. Open Door Policy
l. progressive movement
m. Prohibition
n. socialism
o. social gospel
p. Treaty of Versailles

___ 36. Karl Marx's theory proposing a classless society and government ownership of business.

___ 37. Period when alcoholic drinks were outlawed.

___ 38. Religious movement designed to improve present social conditions.

___ 39. Agreement that punished Germany harshly after World War I.

___ 40. Basis for American relations with countries in the Far East.

___ 41. Theory that living things had a natural origin and that they gradually evolved into the species existing today.

___ 42. International peace organization established after World War I.

___ 43. System for making large numbers of products by using interchangeable parts and assembly lines.

___ 44. Policy of gaining control over foreign territory.

___ 45. Government programs designed to end the Great Depression.

___ 46. Policy of having little to do with foreign nations.

___ 47. People who moved from eastern and southern Europe to the United States in the years 1890 to 1920.

___ 48. Program of alternate service for conscientious objectors in World War II.

___ 49. Campaign promoting reform and change.

___ 50. Long economic downturn from 1929 to 1939.

Part 5

____ 51. Military alliance formed by Western nations in 1949 to oppose communism.

____ 52. International organization to maintain world peace.

____ 53. Conflict without fighting between enemy nations.

____ 54. Barrier to communication and travel between communist nations and free nations.

____ 55. Measure passed in 1956 to build a network of interstate highways.

____ 56. Case in which separate but equal facilities for blacks were declared unconstitutional.

____ 57. Measure that gave President Johnson power to use military force in Vietnam.

____ 58. Title of President Johnson's social programs.

____ 59. Drive to give blacks equal status with whites.

____ 60. Program for conscientious objectors from the 1950s to the 1970s.

a. *Brown v. Board of Education of Topeka*
b. civil rights movement
c. Cold War
d. Great Society
e. Interstate Highway Act
f. Iron Curtain
g. I-W service
h. North Atlantic Treaty Organization
i. Tonkin Gulf Resolution
j. United Nations
k. Warsaw Pact

(60 points)

B. Matching: People

Part 6

a. Alexander Hamilton
b. Christopher Columbus
c. Cornwallis
d. Daniel Boone
e. Eli Whitney
f. Francisco de Coronado
g. George Whitefield
h. Henry Hudson
i. Hernando de Soto
j. Jacques Cartier
k. James Oglethorpe
l. John Cabot
m. John Marshall
n. John Smith
o. Meriwether Lewis
p. Ponce de León
q. Robert de La Salle
r. Robert Fulton
s. Roger Williams
t. Samuel de Champlain
u. William Penn

____ 61. "Admiral of the Ocean Sea" who discovered the New World.

____ 62. Explorer of the northeastern coast of North America for England in 1497.

____ 63. Explored the area of the St. Lawrence River for France in 1534.

____ 64. Spanish explorer who discovered Florida while seeking the Fountain of Youth.

____ 65. Spanish explorer who discovered the Mississippi River in 1541.

____ 66. Spanish explorer who sought the Seven Cities of Cíbola in the Southwest.

____ 67. The "father of New France."

___ 68. Explorer who claimed part of North America for the Netherlands in 1609.

___ 69. Leader of Jamestown who established a policy of "no work, no food."

___ 70. Founder of Rhode Island, who insisted on freedom of conscience.

___ 71. Quaker who received a land grant as payment for a debt.

___ 72. Trustee leader in the founding of Georgia.

___ 73. Leader of the colonial religious revival in the 1700s.

___ 74. British general who surrendered in the last major battle of the American Revolution.

___ 75. Man who explored the Louisiana Purchase from 1804 to 1806.

___ 76. Man who opened the Wilderness Road to Kentucky.

___ 77. Man who built the first successful steamboat, the *Clermont*.

___ 78. Chief justice who strengthened the Supreme Court in the early 1800s.

___ 79. Inventor of the cotton gin.

___ 80. Federalist leader and first secretary of the treasury.

Part 7

a. Alexander Graham Bell
b. Andrew Carnegie
c. Booker T. Washington
d. Douglas MacArthur
e. Dred Scott
f. Dwight L. Moody
g. George Custer
h. Jefferson Davis
i. John D. Rockefeller
j. Marcus Whitman
k. Martin Luther King, Jr.
l. Noah Webster
m. Robert E. Lee
n. Samuel F. B. Morse
o. Samuel Slater
p. Stephen Austin
q. Thomas Edison
r. Wright brothers

___ 81. Inventor of the telegraph.

___ 82. Brought textile manufacturing to America.

___ 83. Man who began colonizing Texas.

___ 84. Missionary who encouraged settlement of Oregon.

___ 85. President of the Confederate States of America.

___ 86. Chief general of the Confederate armies.

___ 87. Black man whose appeal for freedom was rejected by the Supreme Court.

___ 88. Black leader who founded Tuskegee Institute.

___ 89. Colonel defeated at the Battle of the Little Bighorn in 1876.

___ 90. Man who invented a practical electric light bulb.

___ 91. Man who invented the telephone.

___ 92. Famous evangelist in the latter half of the 1800s.

___ 93. Man who founded Standard Oil as the first trust.

___ 94. Man whose company helped to make the United States a leading steel producer.

___ 95. Made the first successful flight with a heavier-than-air machine in 1903.

___ 96. General who served in World War II and the Korean War, and was dismissed by President Truman.

___ 97. Black minister who led the civil rights movement and promoted nonviolent resistance.

Part 8 (Presidents of 1789–1849)

___ 98. First president; 1789–1797.

___ 99. President during War of 1812; 1809–1817.

___ 100. President during the Era of Good Feelings; 1817–1825.

___ 101. Son of a former president; 1825–1829.

___ 102. First vice president to fill the position of a president who died in office; 1841–1845.

___ 103. Leader of the Democratic-Republicans; third president; 1801–1809.

___ 104. Second president; Federalist; 1797–1801.

___ 105. First president to die in office; 1841.

___ 106. President who represented the common man; 1829–1837.

___ 107. Former vice president under Andrew Jackson; 1837–1841.

a. Andrew Jackson
b. George Washington
c. James K. Polk
d. James Madison
e. James Monroe
f. John Adams
g. John Quincy Adams
h. John Tyler
i. Martin Van Buren
j. Thomas Jefferson
k. William Henry Harrison

Part 9 (Presidents of 1849–1901)

___ 108. President when the Compromise of 1850 passed; 1850–1853.

___ 109. President when Southern states began to secede; 1857–1861.

___ 110. President during the Civil War; 1861–1865.

___ 111. President impeached in 1868; 1865–1869.

___ 112. Former Civil War general; 1869–1877.

___ 113. President appointed after a disputed election; 1877–1881.

___ 114. President assassinated after only a few months in office; 1881.

___ 115. Became president when the former president was assassinated; 1881–1885.

___ 116. Only president to serve two nonconsecutive terms; 1885–1889 and 1893–1897.

___ 117. President during the Spanish-American War; was assassinated; 1897–1901.

a. Abraham Lincoln
b. Andrew Johnson
c. Benjamin Harrison
d. Chester Arthur
e. Grover Cleveland
f. James Buchanan
g. James Garfield
h. Millard Fillmore
i. Rutherford B. Hayes
j. Ulysses S. Grant
k. William McKinley

Part 10 (Presidents of 1901–2000)

____ 118. President of the New Freedom program; served during World War I; 1913–1921.

____ 119. President of the Square Deal and the "big stick"; 1901–1909.

____ 120. President when United States troops withdrew from Vietnam; first president to resign; 1969–1974.

____ 121. President elected in 1960 and assassinated in 1963.

____ 122. President of the New Deal; served during World War II; only one to serve more than two terms; 1933–1945.

____ 123. President who brought economic recovery in the 1980s; 1981–1989.

____ 124. President during most of the 1950s; 1953–1961.

____ 125. Vice president who became president in 1963 and was re-elected in 1964; promoted the Great Society; 1963–1969.

____ 126. President who replaced Franklin Roosevelt; ordered use of the atomic bomb; promoted the Fair Deal; 1945–1953.

____ 127. President when the Cold War ended and the Persian Gulf War was fought; 1989–1993.

a. Calvin Coolidge
b. Dwight D. Eisenhower
c. Franklin D. Roosevelt
d. George H. W. Bush
e. Harry S. Truman
f. John F. Kennedy
g. Lyndon B. Johnson
h. Richard M. Nixon
i. Ronald Reagan
j. Theodore Roosevelt
k. Woodrow Wilson

(67 points)

C. Matching: Dates

a. 1588
b. 1607
c. 1620
d. 1733
e. 1763
f. July 4, 1776
g. 1775–1783
h. 1787
i. 1789
j. 1861–1865
k. 1877
l. 1898
m. 1914–1918
n. 1939–1945
o. 1941
p. 1950–1953
q. 1973

____ 128. Treaty of Paris after the French and Indian War.

____ 129. World War II.

____ 130. Declaration of Independence signed.

____ 131. Korean War.

____ 132. World War I.

____ 133. Jamestown founded.

____ 134. Georgia founded.

____ 135. Spanish Armada defeated.

____ 136. Plymouth Colony founded.

____ 137. Pearl Harbor attacked.

____ 138. American Revolution.

____ 139. Beginning of government under the Constitution.

____ 140. United States withdrawal from Vietnam.

____ 141. Constitutional Convention.

____ 142. Spanish-American War.

____ 143. Civil War.

(16 points)

D. True or False

Circle T for True or F for False.

T F 144. Columbus thought he could reach the East by sailing west.

T F 145. One reason that the Spanish built missions was to protect their frontier against foreign nations.

T F 146. The Spanish operated their missions on the basis of democracy and freedom, and treated the Indians fairly and respectfully.

T F 147. The economic prosperity of New France depended on the fur trade.

T F 148. Pennsylvania was founded as a place of freedom for Catholics.

T F 149. The Carolinas were to be modeled on the feudal system.

T F 150. The Puritans came to America for religious freedom but would not grant full religious freedom to others.

T F 151. Jamestown was settled primarily for religious freedom.

T F 152. Colonial charters granted colonists the same privileges as Englishmen.

T F 153. Shipping and manufacturing were more important in the South than in New England.

T F 154. The Bible had little effect on people living in early colonial days.

T F 155. The French and Indian War is important in history because the French were removed as a power in North America.

T F 156. The Americans and British disagreed about Parliament's authority over the colonies.

T F 157. The Constitution, like the laws of the Medes and Persians, may never be changed.

T F 158. The purpose of the Bill of Rights is to guarantee freedoms to citizens of the United States.

T F 159. The American republic has no king and is a pure democracy.

T F 160. President Jefferson increased the size of the government.

T F 161. State nullification of federal laws would have led to chaos and breakup of national unity.

T F 162. Andrew Jackson opposed the Bank of the United States because he believed it favored the wealthy and was unconstitutional.

T F 163. The cotton gin helped to firmly establish slavery in the South.

T F 164. Industry grew rapidly in the North because of energy, natural resources, and transportation.

T F 165. The Erie Canal served to divert much trade away from New Orleans to New York City.

T F 166. The Civil War began as a war to free the slaves.

T F 167. Lincoln's assassination was a great loss to both the North and the South.

T F 168. The Radical Republicans wanted to make blacks and whites equal by law.

T F 169. Southern states passed black codes to aid the blacks' adjustment to freedom.

T F 170. The Homestead Act encouraged settlement of the West by providing cheap or free land.

T F 171. The cattle kingdom had little to do with transportation.

T F 172. Greed was a chief cause of the Indian wars.

T F 173. Labor unions are inconsistent with the Bible doctrine of nonresistance and with the Scriptural approach to working.

T F 174. Darwin's theory of evolution had wide influence.

T F 175. Progressive educators changed the schools to be more traditional.

T F 176. Immigrants made only a few contributions to the United States.

T F 177. The imperialism of the 1890s marked a significant shift from the isolationism of the previous thirty years.

T F 178. The United States actively tried to help the territories it had conquered.

T F 179. Progressive reformers believed that social problems resulted from man's sinful condition.

T F 180. At the peace conference at Paris after World War I, Woodrow Wilson wanted to harshly punish Germany while the other Allied leaders wanted to be more lenient.

T F 181. The Republican presidents of the 1920s increased government regulation of business.

T F 182. The New Deal helped to shorten the Great Depression.

T F 183. The Mennonite Church did little for the benefit of conscientious objectors in World War II.

T F 184. Supreme Court decisions in the 1960s allowed Bible reading and prayer in public schools.

T F 185. The United States faced economic problems in the 1970s.

T F 186. An economic expansion began in the middle 1980s.

T F 187. The Cold War ended when Communist governments of Eastern Europe fell during 1989 and 1990.

(44 points)
Total points: 187